HORSEMANSHIP MADE EASY:

Lunging

Samantha Fletcher

To my husband,
Jeff Fletcher, the best editor and partner anyone
could ask for.

My Mother,
Who gave me the passion for writing and teaching
and I ran with it.

My Friends,
Taylor and Stephanie for keeping me focused,

And Student, Nina Gertzman, for helping with
demonstrations and handling.

To Our Readers:

Horsemanship Made Easy advises all readers to take notes (the key points at the end of each chapter) and bring these notes out to the arena with them. Index cards work great for this! Everyone forgets things when it's time to apply what you've read, so don't take the chance and bring the Key Points along with you!

Table of Contents

Introduction

Have you ever walked an unruly dog? They pull. And pull. And they will continue to pull until you change your actions.

Introducing your horse to lunging. Where to Start.

Lunging a horse is much the same. Your horse will do its best to run the show. Until you change your actions.

Any horseman who has spent time around our hooved friends knows that lunging a horse can look like a work of art, or like a pair of clowns playing tug of war. Truly learning how to communicate with your horse, and understanding their body language, comes with time. Time spent both in the saddle and on the ground. Too much of one or the other often leads to misunderstandings and miscommunication.

Horses are fight or flight animals. They are very strong and easily able to hurt us. If at any time you are uncertain with your ability to perform these exercises with your horse _HIRE A TRAINER_. Your safety and that of your horse is first and foremost. If you think your horse is dangerous, it probably is. This book is not meant to replace a professional horse trainer when dealing with a dangerous horse.

Let's go over a few key aspects of lunging and ground work, explain the basic body language of your horse, and have you and your horse looking like an artful dance.

Basic Principle of Lunging

Many horse owners skip ground work. This is a huge mistake. It's like going to the doctor and having them guess why you are there. Lunging your horse will tell you its symptoms, its strengths and its weaknesses. At some point in your experience working with equines you will find yourself needing this skill. In my teaching and with my personal horses, at the very least the first week is spent on the ground, evaluating each one and seeing their short comings.

Lunging in a round pen is helpful for every discipline, and for any horse. Proper lunging will let you see things you might otherwise have missed under saddle. Most behavioral problems can be fixed by various applications of ground work, usually in a round pen. Many riders scoff and find ground work boring, until they see how quickly and solidly an issue can be addressed on the ground.

This book will discuss the basics aspects of lunging, what to look for while lunging, and some common issues that occur during lunging. Keep in mind that many holes in a horse's behavior under saddle are often because trainers have skipped some part of groundwork.

Yes, lunging is basically sending your horse in circles at different gaits.

No, you should not be chasing and whipping your horse the entire time.

Any horse can learn how to lunge quietly. It's not a matter of inability; it is a matter of how long the person is willing to take to get that quiet, respectful horse. Notice I used the word respectful, not fearful. Each horse is different and will need a different amount of work. Even more importantly, use a different level of pressure. A sensitive horse may require very little pressure. That horse may respond to the simplest change in your body language. A lazy horse may require more pressure.

Always remember....... Horses learn from the release of pressure, not the pressure itself!

Key point: Only use the least amount of pressure necessary.

Clear Cues, Quick Results

Lunging is, in effect, mimicking the behavior of a lead stallion or mare in a herd. We are moving the horse's feet to establish ourselves as the dominant horse in our partnership. Doing this once or twice won't create this respect; rather it should be a consistent practice and new aspect of your regular routine. You won't need to lunge every time you work with your hose after your position is well established, but it will need to be reestablished regularly to create the respectful relationship between you and your horse.

Clear, concise cues and consistency are the keys to communicating effectively with your horse. Speaking horse body language is the first step to a quality partnership with any horse. Lunging is the foundation, an explanation of boundaries and rules the horse will be expected to follow. This is done first in the round pen then reinforced during daily handling. The basic principle to show the horse these "ground rules" is to give a horse steady increase in pressure until they give you the desired behavior. Then to IMMEDIANTLY remove the pressure, at the precise moment the horse behaved as asked. Once again remember.....horses learn from the release of pressure, not the pressure itself.

Nina, pointing in the direction she wants Bella to turn towards.

For example, if you point in the desired direction, for them to move out (we'll call this "one") count to one Mississippi. If the horse doesn't move in that direction, then cluck or kiss (this would be "two"), and they still don't move out you'd then increase to a whip or shake of the tail of the line behind the horse's rump. If that doesn't work, you guessed it, you increase the pressure. Some people are very sensitive (and rightly so) to how much pressure they use on their horse. You shouldn't jump from "one" to "three", always increase steadily. And always REMOVE the pressure as soon as the desired behavior is achieved.   If the horse responds to your pointing in the direction you desire them to move, DON'T cluck and DON'T use the whip.

The goal is to obtain the desired behavior at the lease amount of pressure (pointing). And believe me, your horse will achieve this, but NOT if you keep upping the pressure without giving the horse a chance to respond. Reward the try. Reward the behavior.

Key Points:
- Increase Pressure slowly
- Don't "Jump" or "Skip" pressure levels

REMOVE THE PRESSURE AS SOON AS THE HORSE RESPONDS CORRECTLY

Understanding Body Language:

Your Own and Your Horse's

As humans, we use body language daily without really noticing. Hunch shoulders and a downward gaze denote an unsure or unconfident person, while shoulders back and a smile show the opposite. These small differences in a person's posture give us an idea of how they will react in a conversation, but most of our communication is done through words.

Horses don't have the luxury of verbal speech. The most you'll hear from them might be a call or a nicker, but besides these MOST of their communication comes from body language. Just as you might be able to tell if a dog is friendly or scared by the position of head, tail and ears, you can learn this silent language horses use.

Bella, displaying angry body language. Note the pinned ears, furrowed nostrils and swishing tail.

Horses have a language among themselves. You need to speak that same language. Your horse isn't going to learn English. He isn't going to behave just because you love him. Horses don't respond to bribery. Ever. Bribe your horse with treats and you will soon own a dominate horse. I'm not saying don't give your horse treat. But don't confuse your dog's behavior with your horse's. Your dog might do a trick in anticipation of a treat. Your horse will NOT exhibit this same behavior. The horse will see you offering his treat as you giving up your food. He directed your action. This is why many horse owners do not give treats by hand but rather will drop them in the horse's feed bucket.

Note the behavior of horses in a paddock at dinner time. The dominant horse in the herd hierarchy is not going to take a lazy head bob of a 'lower' horse when they tell him to move off their food. They will bite or kick and I promise *they* are going to do it with a lot more pressure than a person can manage with a whip.

The dominant horse moves the lower horse's feet.

The dominant horse controls the lower horse's action.

THIS IS IMPORTANT: **The dominant horse moves the lower horse's feet. The dominate horse did not offer a treat to the other horse to get them to move.**

This means if your horse is making you move (either by crowding your space or more aggressive tactics) YOU are the lower horse. And you do not want a thousand pound animal thinking they can treat you like their lower herd mate.

Body Language Basics

The main parts of the body to watch are head position, ear position and hip position.

Being prey animals, a horse's body language is not the same as a predator's might be (i.e. dogs, humans and so on). As you start to watch for these more basic aspects of their body language, you will begin to see more subtle cues like facial expressions (Yes! Horses do have facial expressions!).

Head position is the first major indicator of a horse trying to speak to you. An outstretched nose, attempting to smell you is good. While a high head denotes fear or uncertainty. A fearful horse lifts its heads to keep it away from predators and find a way out of the situation they feel trapped in. We are predators, we smell like predators, we move like predators, and most often a person's first instinct when greeting a horse is to reach for its face. Instead, greet a new horse first allowing them to smell you, then, if they are willing, with a scratch on the withers, just as they would greet each other. This is the part of their body they will most often accept touch first.

The next aspect to watch for is the horse's ear position. Horses are very expressive with them, whether they are pinned flat against their skull, which shows anger and aggression, or pricked in attention searching for the source of a sound. Horses have an interesting aspect of ear position and eye focus. Because of their rectangular pupil, each eye of a horse can see one hundred and eighty degrees (minus a small blind spot in front of their nose and directly behind their tail dock). Each side of the horse's ear and eyes work independently, so where their left ear is pointed their left eye is focused, where their right ear goes their right eye does as well. This is great for seeing predators sneaking up on them, finding a way out of a precarious position, or spooking at things that might be a predator (or could be a plastic bag stuck to a bush). So, unless they are pinning their ears, you can note what your horse is focusing on by their ear position.

Hip position. This is the most important body pos cue to pay attention to on the ground. Hip position migh strange at first, but it will keep you much safer if you wa... it. The position a horse puts its hip in relation to the person, or other horse, near it shows whether that horse sees that person or animal as a threat, or a leader. The hip, and hind legs of a horse is where all the power is held, and is their most effective weapon. If a horse positions its hip towards you while you work it in a round pen or if they turn their rump towards you while you are attempting to catch him in a turnout, he is disrespecting you, and this is putting you in danger.

A gelding (the 1st Horse) aiming his hip at another horse, which is invading his space. The gelding has his ears pinned, nostrils furrowed and his hip aimed at the 2nd horse. The 2nd horse raises its head to avoid the kick, and is stopping to change direction.

How to Talk Back

This is the hardest part for people to learn: your body language is already speaking to your horse. You have to police yourself here. You have to exude confidence, and claim your personal space around your horse. Square your shoulders. Walk with purpose. And most importantly do not let your horse enter your space without you inviting them in.

Your horse is wired to constantly test the dominant horses in its herd (in small and big ways) for the safety of the herd. If your herd is only you and your horse, that means he will be testing you. Usually these tests start out small, with a crowding of the space when you're tossing your horses breakfast, or a rough shove at your pocket where you keep cookies. If you allow this rude behavior it WILL escalate.

I have seen many horses allowed to continue small rude behaviors until they turn into very dangerous ones. A thousand pounds of muscle can hurt a human without meaning to. Preventing an escalation of rude behaviors will make that horse respect your space from the start and never allow you to get into one of those dangerous situations.

This doesn't mean that you can't have a close relationship with your horse. They don't take it personally when another horse tells them they're being too pushy. They change their approach, and a few moments later are happily grazing or grooming with each other. They don't get upset, they won't hate you for telling them no, and they will in fact feel safer around you when they know they can trust you to keep the scary things at bay.

Your body language will speak much more clearly to your horse than your words. I've spent entire days not saying more than a couple words while working with other trainers (and those words most often are Whoa or the like). You need to be confident and stern at times. Your space is yours. Your horse must be invited into it and never allowed to take it from you. This could be as simple at swatting at their nose when they shove you too roughly for a treat, or as big as moving them around their stall with your body language until they give you space to feed them.

Note Nina's confident body posture: Eyes up and squared shoulders.

The Most Common Problem with Lunging

We've all seen it. After a long day at work you go collect your horse from its stall and make the walk to the turnout. The second you start heading that way you can already see the dust cloud coming from the round pen. That other boarder that you never see riding is out there chasing their horse around in circles, constantly twirling a lunge whip while talking on their cellphone and looking bored. Their chubby gelding is running flat out around the outside of the pen, making a swirling mess of dust from the barely watered ground.

Sadly, when most people think of lunging this is what comes to mind.

Most often, when I am encountered with a horse and owner who have problems with ground work it stems from miscommunication. The most common problem with lunging is just this: The owner is putting too much pressure on the horse, or not releasing it at the right time.

To get a horse from this frantic run, to a well-choreographed dance doesn't happen overnight, but it will happen if you take the necessary time and do your homework. I've taken multiple "crazy barrel horses" and turned them into the most reliable horse on the ranch, by implementing good ground work and reinforcing that work under saddle.

It all comes from release of pressure. Everything a horse learns is from pressure and the release of that pressure. The quicker you release it when they do the right thing, the quicker they will learn whatever you are trying to teach them.

The out of control horse in the above scenario, running haphazardly around and around is being pressured by the owner unknowingly. The constant twirling movement of the whip can do two things. It can sack the horse out, so that it doesn't think it needs to work or move, or in this case it causes an overload of pressure and the horse tries to get away from it by constantly moving. We don't want our horse to do either of these things. The horse should respect your tool (the whip) when you use it, but not be fearful of it.

The way we do this is release the pressure when the horse does the correct response to your cue. You have to be very quick in your release of pressure. You must also be equally quick in reprimanding your horse when they do something wrong.

Where to Start

Let's repeat the three basic body language cues your horse will exhibit. Head position. Ear Position. Hind quarter position. Pay very close attention to these three body cues.

Where do you start? With a horse I know, or have worked with before, I normally recommend to start with the horse on a lunge line or halter. This may not always be the best first step however. If your horse is high spirited, underworked, or just has no clue what you're asking him to do, letting him run and get some of his energy out first may be best. This can be done in a turnout, a large arena, or even the round pen.

After a few sessions of ground work you might not need to turn your horse out before starting to school him. But it's not a bad idea. The more they run around, and burn off some steam, the less energy they'll have to act out.

After turning your horse out, halter and bring them into the round pen. If you don't have one available, a lunge line will work as well. The first step is to ask the horse to "yield" or move his hip away from you.

Nina asks the horse to bend its head, before asking the horse to yield its hind quarters.

Start by moving to his left side. Standing about even with the heart girth, or where your cinch would be if the horse was saddled, place your right hand on his withers. With your left hand take the slack out of the lunge line or lead, bending their nose toward you slightly. When the horse brings his nose towards you, release the slack back to him, rewarding him bending his nose towards you.

After he has bent his nose towards you a few times with minimal amount of pulling on your part, you will keep the bend in his neck, and put pressure on his hind left hip.

Nina applies pressure to the horse's hip, with its head bent towards her, while walking towards the hip.

Remember, use the least amount of pressure first and slowly increase the amount of pressure until he moves his hip away from you. With most horses, a cluck or a spin of the end of the lead rope aimed at the point of his stifle will be sufficient to get them to move off. If you don't know the horse, or are nervous, it is best to use a whip or clinician's stick to give you more reach, and keep you out of kicking distance when starting with this.

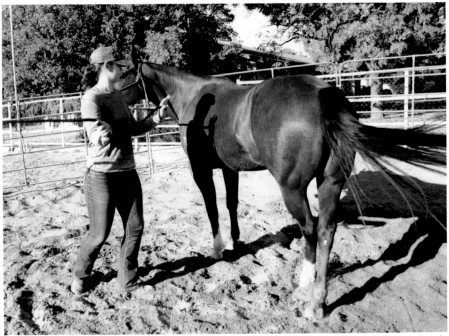

Release pressure after the horse yields its hip (or moves its hip away)

Even if you are using a whip, however, make sure you start with the least amount of pressure (you clucking) then increase to a touch of the whip, a tapping of the whip, and gently increase the amount of force behind the tapping whip. With pressure your horse should step sideways. If he doesn't, increase the pressure. Release the pressure (stop swinging the line or tapping with the stick) *immediately when he moves away*. This is important, because the quicker you reward the horse, the quicker they will make the connection between you placing pressure toward them, and them moving away from that pressure to get release.

After you have successfully moved your horse's hip to their right and away from you a few times, you'll need to repeat the exercise on the other side of the horse's body. Treat each side as a completely different horse, and assume they have no idea what you're asking until you get the desired response on the new side.

This yield the hind quarters exercise should be repeated every time you handle your horse for at least ten sessions before your horse will really grasp the concept. Some horses pick up faster than others, but ten sessions with good quick releases of pressure on your end when the horse responds correctly will make certain they understand your cues. Practice and consistency is key. After your horse learns that they cannot press their hip into you to get you to move, you are ready to move to the next step.

Disengagement is when the horse crosses its legs one over the other as shown above. This makes it difficult for the horse to moves forward quickly and is a form of submission.

Lunging Your Horse around You

Contrary to what it often looks like, you will not be just standing at the center of your horse's circle. You will instead be walking at them, towards their drive line, (see Figure 11) in a smaller circle than the horse is on, and directing their pace, gait and responses with body you language.

The white line denotes the horse's drive line. If the handler is putting pressure on the horse behind the driveline, the horse will move forward. If the handler moves pressure in front of the drive line the horse will stop or turn.

We will focus on free lunging, or lunging a horse off line in a round pen. To let your horse off the halter, you will start with bending his nose towards you and untying the halter. Use the lead of the halter to apply pressure on your horse. Step to the opposite side of which you want him to move in (if you want him to move off to the left, you will step to the right behind his drive line). As you step behind his drive line, point in the direction you want him to move towards, cluck and wave your arm and lead line behind his rump to send him away from where you are standing.

Hold onto the halter until you have moved him a safe distance away. If he turns his rump towards you or moves towards you, swing the halter and lead at him. If he doesn't move away, then increase pressure (whack him with the line) until he moves away. When he yields you space, you can drop the halter outside of the fence of the round pen and pick up your lunge whip. Now, move to the center of the round pen.

You will need to place pressure BEHIND the horse's drive line (see Figure 11 above) in order to get the horse to move forward. Do this by positioning yourself behind the horse's driveline, with the whip pointing behind the horse's rump. Point your arm that is not holding the whip behind his rump, in the direction you want the horse to move towards.

This will create the basis (or Level 1) of pressure for the horse to move forward in the round pen. Note: you are not swinging the whip yet.

The white line denotes the driveline.

Note: Nina's focus and body position is behind the driveline. The whip is kept behind the horse's rump, but it is not waving in the air, because this horse moved out with only the pressure of Nina's eyes and whip on the ground behind the horse.

IF you place pressure behind the horse's driveline (positioning the whip behind the horse, not whipping the air, and not whipping the horse's rump) and the horse does not move forward, you would increase pressure by walking towards the drive line and gently swinging the whip at the air behind the horse. The increase of pressure, remember, should be incremental, and the pressure should stop as soon as the horse shows the desired behavior (note in image above that Nina has released pressure, because the horse did move out).

Again, if the horse does not move forward when you step behind the driveline and move the whip behind his rump, then increase to a point of the hand (in the direction you want the horse to move in) and a verbal cue (a cluck for a trot or a kiss for a canter). If the horse does not respond to the verbal cue increase to swinging the whip, and increase from there to cracking the whip behind the horse. If the horse still does not move out, and you can reach him with the lunge whip smack his rump. It's important to note that if you can reach your horse with the lunge whip he is being disrespectful. He is not moving out of your space and pressure should be increase until he moves away from you (i.e. smacking his rump with the whip.

Remember: always release pressure when the horse shows the desired behavior as soon as the horse shows the desired behavior. The quicker you *release* pressure (and reward the horse) the quicker your horse will learn what you are *asking* with the cue (pressure).

Key Point: Pay attention to your horse's hip when you release him or send him off away from you. DO NOT let him aim it at you, and make sure you have room to get back away if he kicks out when moving forward. Even if he doesn't mean to hurt you horses will often kick out when let off line out of glee or for fun. Even though they may be playing they could seriously hurt you.

Where to Apply the Pressure

To get your horse to move forward, standing in the center of the round pen, you want to position yourself at his side, and your eyes should be on his heart girth (where your girth or cinch would be if he were saddled). The whip should behind his rump (See Image above). This places the pressure behind him and tells him to move forward away from it. Unless he stops moving you should have the whip trailing behind him on the ground. No absent minded spinning, you don't need to constantly swing it at him. Less is more here.

If your horse stops, tries to turn around, or moves to position his hip at you, apply pressure. Start at the lowest level you need and increase it until you get the desired response. Raise the whip, whip the air, and if you still don't get a response and he doesn't move his feet clip his rump with the whip.

BUT only increase the pressure until they respond and move out. Release pressure (bring the whip down to the relaxed trailing position) as soon as they continue forward.

The whip is meant to replicate a fly biting the horse's rump. Imagine if a horse is sitting in a pasture. A fly lands on their flank, if they don't twitch it off, the fly will crawl around. If they still don't twitch it away the fly will bit them. That's how the whip should be used. We ask with a cluck first, increase pressure to raising the whip. Then increase to whipping the air, then the whip "bites" the horse. Normally, horses will move out before the whip has to be used on their rump. If not, you have to be prepared to use it or the horse will think he doesn't have to respond to you.

Rememeber: We are replicating the behavior horse's use with each other. The lower horse moves his feet. If you ask your horse to move, and he doesn't, he thinks you are the lower horse.

Turning Your Horse

So your horse is moving out around the round pen. The next step is to turn him. The more often we get our horse turning while working in the round pen or on the lunge line, the quicker we wear them out. A tired horse is much easier to handle.

Nina backs away, changes the whip to her opposite hand, points in the direction she wants the horse to turn, steps in front of the horse's drive line, and increases pressure (walking towards the horse infront of its driveline) until the horse turns.

Our main goal is to get our horse to turn quickly, with their head in towards us and their rump to the fence. Because they don't really have a choice of which way to turn on a lunge line (they'd get tangled if they managed to turn toward the outside) we will discuss turning the horse correctly in a round pen without a line first.

Most horses have spent their life being chased around a round pen, so they are much more likely to turn with their nose towards the fence than towards the center. They have been inadvertently taught to run away. What they should be taught is to submit to the person in the round pen.

The reason this is important is that we never want the horse's rump (their main weapon) pointed towards us. If you watch them interact with each other, they do this so they can kick out quickly at the source of pressure if they need to. We don't want them feeling comfortable pointing a weapon at us.

To get your horse to turn towards you, you will back away from the horse dramatically (effectively halving the round pen, and cutting them off). This will place you in front of the horse's "Drive line". The drive line is the imaginary line at their heart girth, if you are behind it, they move forward, if you get in front of it the horse will stop, slowdown or turn. This is the same line that all herd animals have, and how a herding dog moves a herd.

Nina steps back, switches the whip to her other hand, points in the direction she wants the horse to go and puts increasing pressure in front of the driveline (the white line) until the horse turns.

As you are backing up, you will switch the whip to your other hand. The horse will turn when they see you cross in front of their drive line. If your horse turns with his rump towards you, you should immediately (or as soon as possible) back up, cut him off again and turn him around to the original direction he was going. He shouldn't be allowed to take a break, or slow down until he gives you a turn the 'correct' way (facing inward toward you during the turn).

It may take a few sessions before you get even a couple turns toward the inside, because he has been conditioned the other way first. You have to outweigh the number of times they have done something incorrectly with the number of times they do it correctly. This will take time but will make you both safer and happier.

Choosing the Gait

A gait is the way your horse is moving. The three basic gaits are: Walk, Trot and Canter (also called Lope). Horses can have additional gaits (most often seen in 'gaited breeds' like Tennesee walkers, pacers, paso finos and the like), but we will mostly speak about walk, trot, canter here. Each gait can have a subtype. Think of this as slow, medium and fast, within each gait.

Besides the look of the gait, each gait can be described by the number of 'beats', or times they feet or pairs of feet hit the ground.

Walking is a four beat gait. This means you can count out four beats, and each hoof lands on a different beat. If the horse moved its front left hoof first, its hind right would follow, then its front right, followed by its hind left.

Horse at a Walk

Trotting is a two beat gait. The hooves move in diagonal sets. The front left hoof moves with the hind right. The front right hoof syncs with the hind left. When an instructor talks about sitting a "diagonal" they are talking about posting in sync with the rise and fall of the horse's beat at a trot. When a horse is traveling in a circle, to be in synchronization with their balance the rider must "rise and fall with the shoulder on the wall". This means that as the horse brings up its "outside" leg (or the leg that is nearest the fence line) the rider should be in the up position of their post. When that same front leg lands on the ground, the rider should be in the down position of their post, or sitting in the saddle. When the horse changes to the opposite direction circle, the rider would have to change the beat of their post to follow the horse's "diagonal". To do this the rider must sit two "beats" of the horse's trot (or two strides) and rise on the third beat. This will change the diagonal the rider is synchronized with. Image below shows a horse in a trot.

Note the diagonal pairs of legs moving as a set. This is where the term "diagonal" comes from when talking about sitting the beat of a horse's trot.

The Canter or Lope is a three beat gait. If the is traveling to the left, and is on the correct 'lead' (which shoulder is "leading" the canter) he would move his hind right, then his hind left and front right in unison, followed by his left front. (See Image below for a still of the Canter).

Bella demonstrating a canter. The lead shoulder would be the last foot to hit the ground in the sequence of the canter. In this case, she is on the left lead which is the correct lead for her circle.

For visual representations of each gait various videos are available online, with slow motion cameras. I have also provided stills of each gait above. Practice watching your horse's feet. Count the beats of the different gaits.

A horse will have a slow, medium and fast version of each gait. But for now we will mostly want to just get a clear difference between the main three gaits.

The hardest thing to get any horse to when not on a line in a round pen is to simply walk.

It will take some time before you are able to get your horse to walk. Before we can expect them to walk, we must get them to reliably trot off line. Most horses will lunge fairly easily at a canter. If you are able to get your horse to turn reliably and lope off in each direction the next step is to him to slow down into a trot.

To get your horse to slow down, you will need to release pressure. The best way to do this is to back away (not so much that he turns around) and keep more distance between you and him. This is easier said than done. Another way to back off pressure is to "lower" your body language. Lower your shoulders, slow your movements down, lower the whip and back it further behind his rump. Imagine that the distance between you and your horse is a gas pedal. The closer you get to him the more he will speed up. The further away the more he will slow down. You get far enough away and he will eventually stop (and turn).

Just as changing your horse's way of turning will take time, getting him to slow down and relax while being lunged will take time, and patience on your part.

Facing In

To finish each lunging session, we want our horse to come in to us. To do this, you will invite him into your space. The way to do this is back your pressure off, slow down your movements and back away until he stops and looks at you. At first he might turn around but if you hold your ground, he should 'face in' and wait for further instruction.

Nina has gotten Bella to stop. She invites her to come towards her with an open hand and setting the whip on the ground

To invite your horse in to you, hold your hand out, and back away. It may take a moment for him to realize that you aren't going to ask him to work again. If he comes in to your hand, scratch his face, and offer encouraging words.   No, don't give him a treat.

IF your horse DOESN'T come in toward you and instead decides to wander off, eat weeds, or start whining to his friends, you will immediately ask him back up to a trot or lope and work him again, until he gives you his attention. Repeat turns, and trotting, change directions. When he is paying attention again, you can try to stop him and ask him in again. Repeat the process if he tries to wander off again. You have to do this until he comes in, and this might take a while. I've had horses who take five minutes, and others who one lunging session can be as long as an hour or more.

If you are releasing pressure quickly, and reprimanding quickly when needed, each session should be shorter and shorter until they keep their attention on you fully from the start.

Finishing up

After your horse comes to you, I like to try walking away a few steps. If the horse has truly been paying attention they should follow you obediently without the lead on. He should follow you for a few strides happily enjoying his break from work. I would then halter him. If he tries to walk away from you, you must again lunge him, ask him in, and then halter him.

Bella comes towards Nina, competing their lunging session.

I find the best way to end the session is to work on what you started with. In this case, and for the first ten sessions at the very least, this would be repeating the hind end yielding exercise we worked on before we started to lunge him. This gives him the chance to pay better attention and should help with him learning to keep his hip away from you (the dominant "horse").

Congratulations! You have finished a good session of lunging with your horse and made the first step toward working on obedience issues.

Wrap Up

- Horses learn from the release of pressure, not the pressure itself.
- Use the LEAST amount of pressure necessary
- Increase pressure slowly
- Don't "Jump" or "Skip" pressure levels
- Remove the pressure as soon as the horse responds with the desired behavior
- The dominant horse moves the lower horse's feet
- Use your body language rather than your voice to move direct your horse

Lunging is an important tool. It is the basis for starting a horse, and it should be the foundation that all equestrians use to train a respectful horse. Watching a trainer who has built a relationship with their horse is a beautiful dance. One that is earned. We should all strive to create that type of respectful partnership.

Be the leader of your herd. Even if your herd consist of just you and your horse.

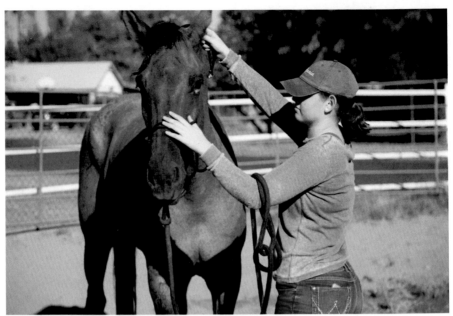

Nina, haltering Kramer after a lunging session.

Recommendations

Thank you for reading! If you've enjoyed this Horsemanship Made Easy Edition check out our other titles at:

- *Horsemanship Made Easy:*

   Transitions

- *Horsemanship Made Easy:*

   How to Buy a Horse the Right Way

About the Author

Samantha Fletcher was born and raised in Arizona. After attending college at Arizona State University and working in the corporate world, she quickly decided that pursuing her love of horses was more rewarding than spread sheets, financial statements and managing employees of different motivation levels.

So, instead, she manages horses of different motivation levels and teaches riding near Peoria, Arizona. Samantha is a multi-award winner in various equine disciplines, including: Cowboy Mounted shooting, Gymkhana, Barrel Racing, Pole Bending, Equitation, English and Western, Trail, Basic Riding, Safety, Jumping, Ground Work and Horsemanship. She can be seen competing in events across Arizona and the South Western US with her mare, Bella.

Her book series "Horsemanship made Easy" can be found on Amazon in either E-book format or as a printed book.

Visit Samantha's Horseback Riding Instruction Website at *AZHorselessons.com* or at her book series Website *HorsemanshipMadeEasy.com*

27864768R00031

Made in the USA
Lexington, KY
06 January 2019